SIMPLE Machines

Nicolas Brasch

Rigby®

www.Rigby.com
1-800-531-5015

Rigby Focus Forward

This Edition © 2009 Rigby, a Harcourt Education Imprint

Published in 2007 by Nelson Australia Pty Ltd ACN: 058 280 149
A Cengage Learning company

1 2 3 4 5 6 7 8 374 14 13 12 11 10 09 08 07
Printed and bound in China

Simple Machines
ISBN-13   978-1-4190-3768-9
ISBN-10   1-4190-3768-4

Acknowledgments
The author and publisher would like to acknowledge permission to reproduce material from the following sources:
Photographs by Alamy/Dave Gibbeson, pp. 3, 6 bottom right, 16, 22, back cover bottom; Fotolia/Sherri Camp, p. 21; Getty Images/AFP/Stan Honda, pp. 6 center right, 8; Getty Images/Dorling Kindersley/Dave King, p. 9 top left; Getty Images/Photodisc Green/ Steve Mason, p. 23; Getty Images/Photonica/Mint Girl Productions, pp. 6 center left, 12; iStockphoto.com, pp. 20 left, back cover center; iStockphoto.com/Daniel Gale, p. 19; iStockphoto.com/Don Wilkie, pp. 7 right, back cover top right; iStockphoto.com/Jim Jurica, p. 15 bottom right; iStockphoto.com/Jonathan Barnes, p. 14 left; iStockphoto. com/Jose Antonio Santiso Fernández, p. 15 bottom left; iStockphoto.com/Julie Elliott, pp. 7, 20; iStockphoto.com/Lisa Fletcher, p. 4; iStockphoto.com/Richard Stouffer, p. 5; Lindsay Edwards, cover, half title page, title page, pp. 9 right, 10, 11, 14 right, 16, 17, 18; Photolibrary/Alamy/Photofusion Picture Library/Christa Stadtler, p. 13; Photolibrary/ Alamy/ mcx images, p. 15 top.

SIMPLE Machines

Nicolas Brasch

Contents

Chapter 1

WHAT IS A MACHINE?

A machine is a tool that makes work easier to do. Machines save people a lot of energy and time.

a crane

a forklift

By using machines, people don't have to push, pull, lift, or carry objects as far or as high as they would without machines.

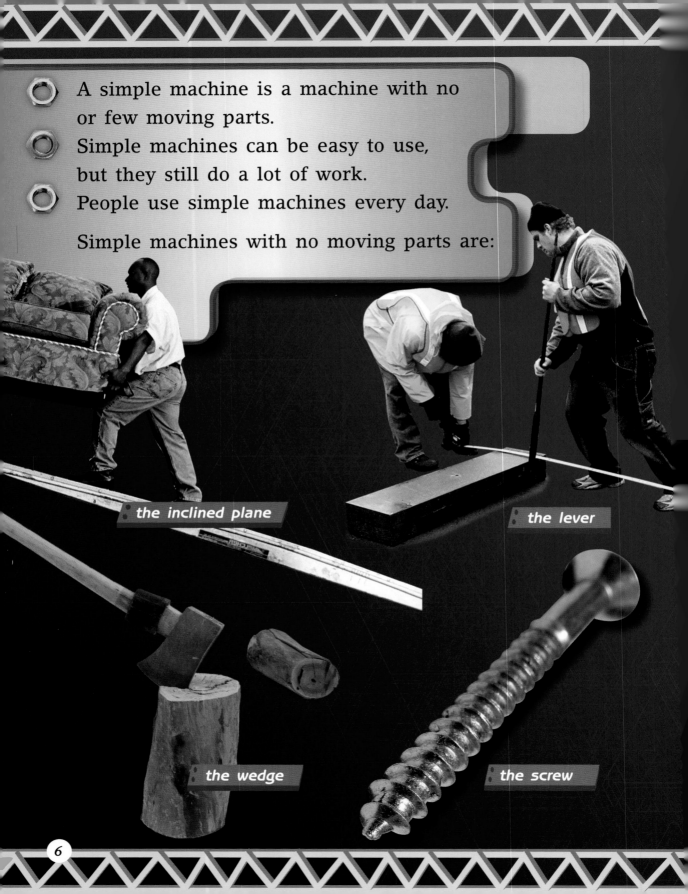

A simple machine is a machine with no or few moving parts.

Simple machines can be easy to use, but they still do a lot of work.

People use simple machines every day.

Simple machines with no moving parts are:

the inclined plane

the lever

the wedge

the screw

Simple machines with moving parts are:

the wheel and axle

the pulley

Chapter 2

THE LEVER

A lever is a simple machine
that can be used to help lift objects
that would normally be too heavy to move easily.

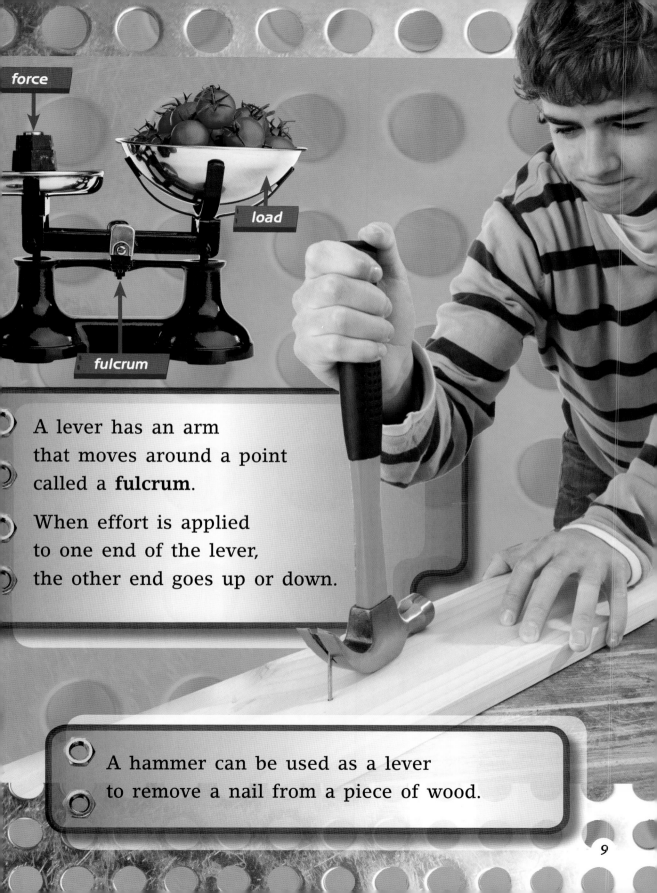

force

load

fulcrum

A lever has an arm
that moves around a point
called a **fulcrum**.

When effort is applied
to one end of the lever,
the other end goes up or down.

A hammer can be used as a lever
to remove a nail from a piece of wood.

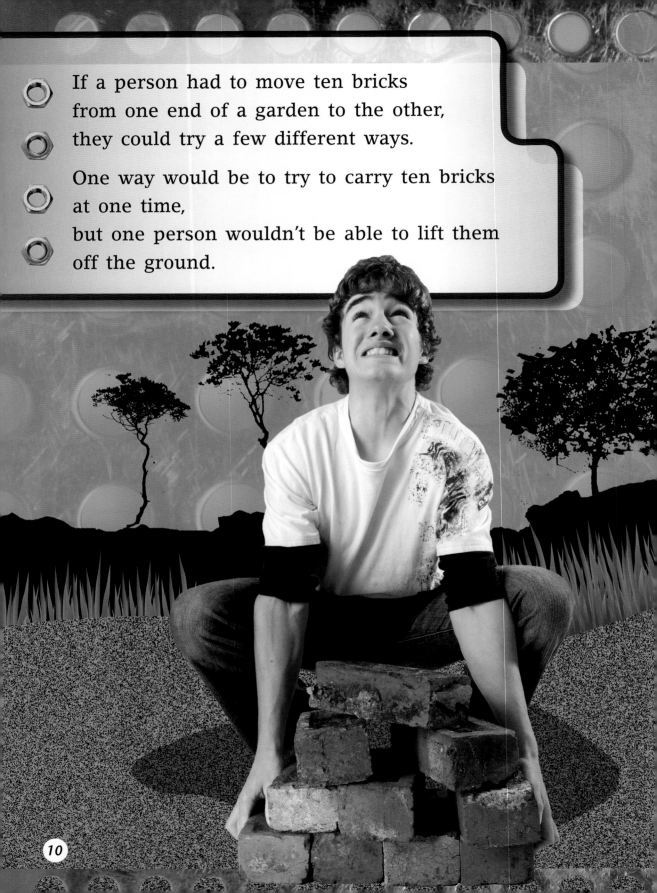

If a person had to move ten bricks
from one end of a garden to the other,
they could try a few different ways.

One way would be to try to carry ten bricks
at one time,
but one person wouldn't be able to lift them
off the ground.

Another way would be to carry the bricks one by one, but this would take a long time.

The best way would be to use a machine with a lever to lift the bricks and then push or pull that machine.

load

force

fulcrum

Chapter 3

THE INCLINED PLANE

A plane is a flat surface.
An inclined plane is an even, sloping surface that joins a lower level to a higher level.

Inclined planes make it easier to move heavy objects from a lower level to a higher level.

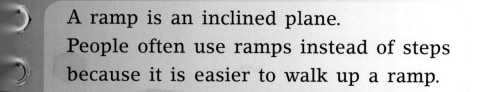

A ramp is an inclined plane.
People often use ramps instead of steps
because it is easier to walk up a ramp.

Ramps are also very useful for people in wheelchairs.

Chapter 4

THE WEDGE

A wedge is made of two inclined planes that are set back-to-back.

People use the pointed edge of a wedge to split things apart.

An ax head is a wedge that can be used to cut through wood.

A chisel is another wedge that cuts through wood. It is usually hit carefully with a hammer to remove one small piece of wood at a time.

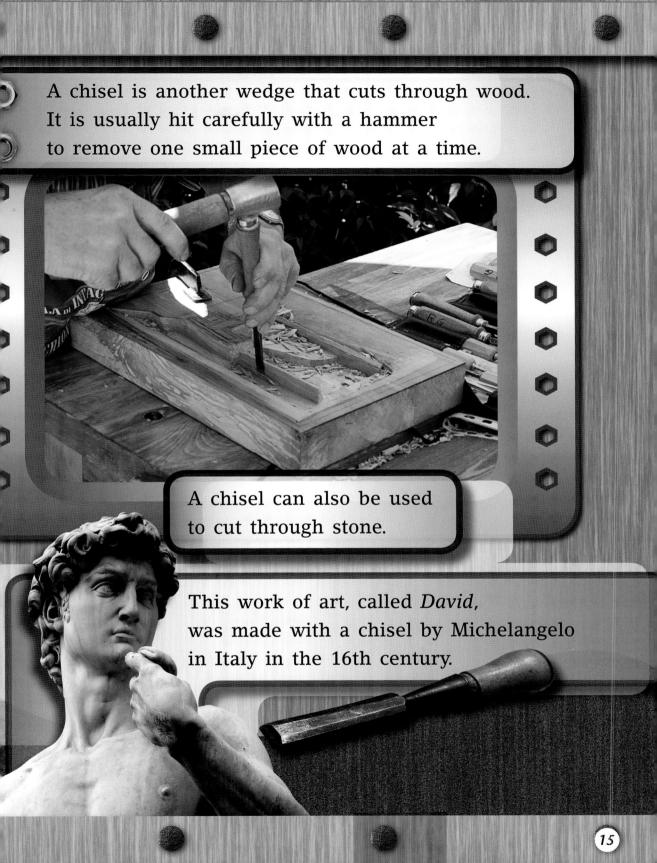

A chisel can also be used to cut through stone.

This work of art, called *David*, was made with a chisel by Michelangelo in Italy in the 16th century.

Chapter 5

THE SCREW

A screw is another type of inclined plane.
It is an inclined plane
wrapped around a cylinder.

inclined plane

right triangle

The longest edge of a **right triangle**
is an inclined plane.

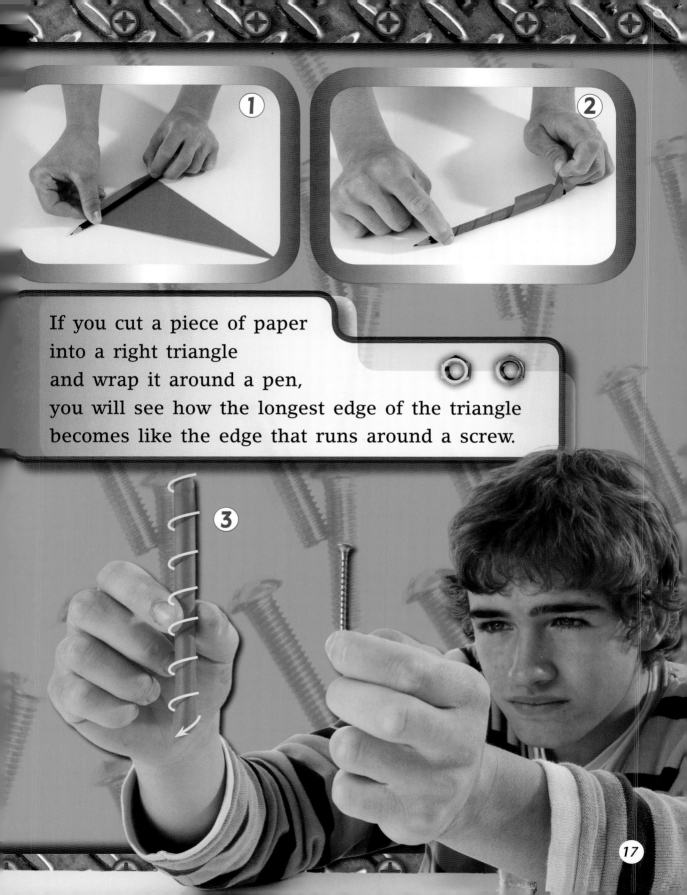

①

②

If you cut a piece of paper
into a right triangle
and wrap it around a pen,
you will see how the longest edge of the triangle
becomes like the edge that runs around a screw.

③

Screws are used to hold objects in place or to hold objects together like glue.

screws

Chapter 6

THE WHEEL AND AXLE

A wheel and **axle** is made up of a larger wheel, or wheels, attached to a smaller wheel, or **shaft**, called an axle.

2 wheel or blades turn

shaft or axle turns **1**

1 axle turn

When either the wheel or axle is turned, the other part also turns, making work easier. The wheel and axle can be found in helicopters, Ferris wheels, and steering wheels.

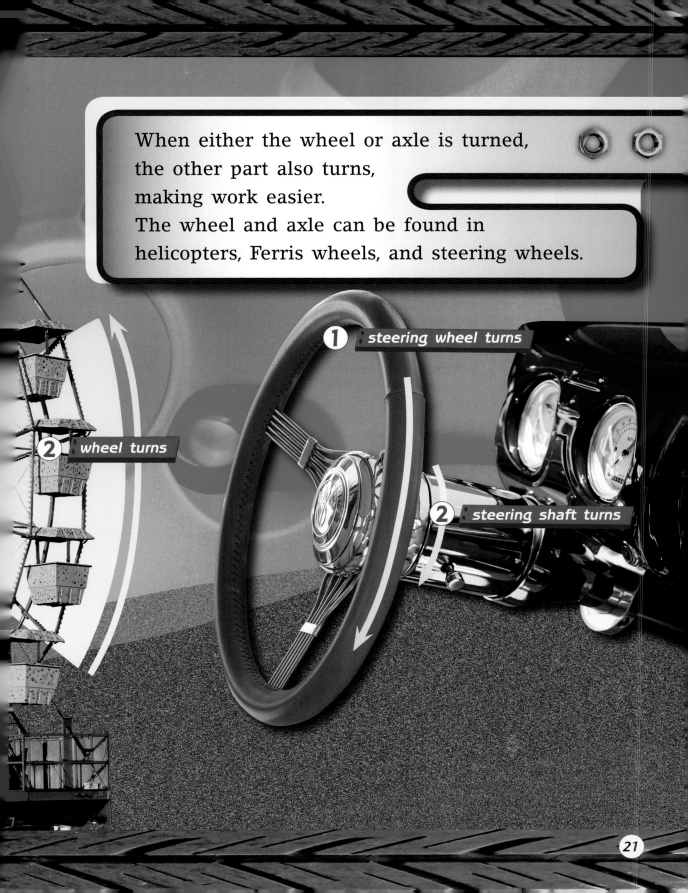

① steering wheel turns

② wheel turns

② steering shaft turns

Chapter 7

THE PULLEY

A pulley is like the wheel and axle. But instead of the wheel being joined to an axle, the wheel has a rope or chain wrapped around it.

At the end of the rope or chain is a hook that can be attached to a heavy object.

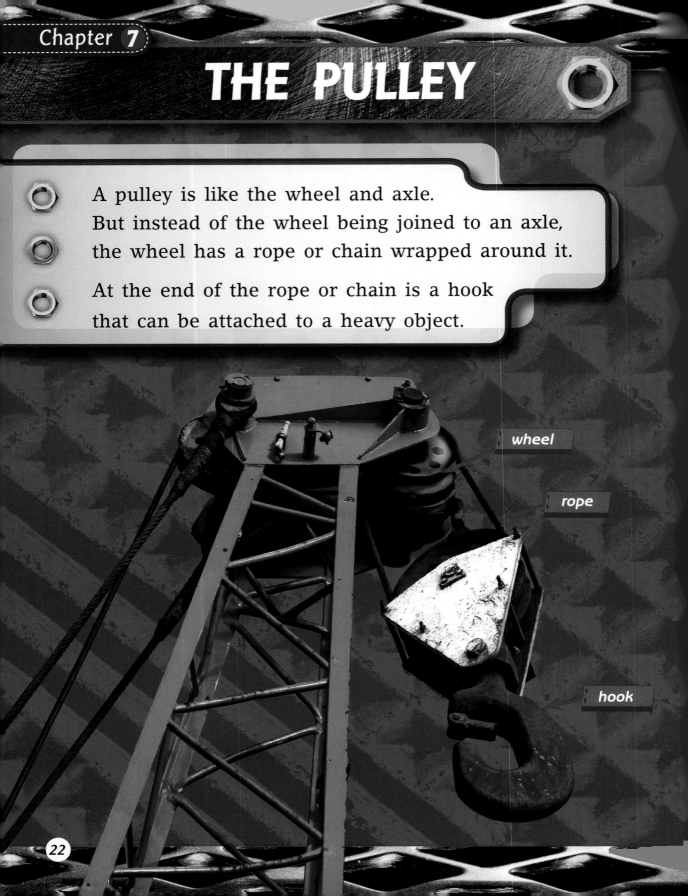

wheel

rope

hook

A pulley is used to lift or lower a heavy object.
As the wheel on the pulley turns,
the rope or chain moves and the heavy object
is lifted or lowered.

With a pulley, one person can lift an object
that it would take many people to lift without a pulley.

rope

wheel

Glossary

axle   a shaft on which one or more wheels is fixed

fulcrum   the point on which a lever turns or is supported

right triangle a triangle in which one corner is a right angle, or a 90° angle

shaft   the stem of a tool

Index